STARS OF THE
NBA

THE COACHES

BY ROBERT ARMSTRONG

CREATIVE EDUCATION/CHILDRENS PRESS

Photography

Jerry Wachter Photography 2, 31, 32, 34, 37
Peter Arnold Photo Archives (Bruce Curtis) 7, 12
Step One Productions 15, 18, 21
Photography, Inc. 23, 25, 26, 28
Axel Studio, Cleveland 41, 45, 46

Published by Creative Educational Society, Inc., 123 South Broad Street, Mankato, Minnesota 56001. Copyright © 1977 by Creative Educational Society, Inc. International copyrights reserved in all countries. No part of this book may be reproduced in any form without written permission from the publisher. Printed in the United States.

Library of Congress Cataloging in Publication Data

Armstrong, Robert, 1938-
  The coaches.

  SUMMARY: Focuses on the relationship between basketball coaches, Red Holzman, Bill Fitch, K.C. Jones, Bill Sharman, and Al Attles, and their respective NBA teams.
  1. Basketball coaching—Juvenile literature. 2. Basketball coaches—United States—Biography—Juvenile literature. 3. National Basketball Association—Juvenile literature. [1. Basketball coaches. 2. National Basketball Association] I. Title.
GV885.3.A84   796.32′3′0922 [B] [920]   76-45181
ISBN 0-87191-566-9

CONTENTS

RED HOLZMAN

When Red Holzman took over as coach of the New York Knicks in December 1967, he told reporters: "I don't think I'm going to be any kind of genius. I don't think I've ever done anything spectacular or really smart. Just the best I could."

If any of the other coaches in the National Basketball Association (NBA) paid any attention to those words, they were in for a rude awakening. When Holzman took over as interim coach from Dick McGuire, the Knicks had a 15-23 record, one percentage point out of last place. For the rest of the season, under Holzman, the Knicks went 28-17, finished third in the East Division and made the play-offs. Holzman was asked to return for another year.

Two years later the Knicks began a five-year period in which they were the best team in pro basketball, perhaps one of the best in history. In that stretch the team

won two NBA championships, and lost a third when two starters were hurt in the final series against Los Angeles.

The difference in the team was not the doing only of Holzman, but it started there. He brought to the team a thorough knowledge of the game, gained as a player under Nat Holman at City College of New York. He was also a solid backcourt performer for eight seasons with the Rochester Royals, was coach for three seasons with the Milwaukee/St. Louis Hawks, and was chief scout for the Knicks for nine years.

Now after nine years on the Knicks' bench, Holzman is recognized as one of the best coaches the league has ever had. He is second only to Red Auerbach in most wins ever for an NBA coach. And though the Knicks have been in decline for two seasons, it is hard to imagine anyone else as their coach.

For what Holzman did with the Knicks was change the whole concept of the way the game was played. From a game in which teams had depended almost solely on the physical abilities of their players, Holzman changed to one which depended on strategy, technique, and teamwork.

Born in 1920 in Brooklyn, Holzman learned his basketball on the city's playgrounds and at Franklin K. Lane High School. But it was not until college, under Holman, that he began to develop. Holzman's coaching philosophy includes a great many things he learned from Holman.

"Holman was an excellent coach," Holzman has said. "He taught you the whole game: how to move without the ball on offense, how to stay between your man and the basket on defense and to know where he was at all times, how to develop an over-all awareness of what was taking place out there on the court — all the other things.

"To put it a different way, Holman taught his players the kind of advanced basketball that would stand them in good stead in the event they might want to go into pro ball."

When Holzman took over as Knicks coach he became the ninth headman in the team's 23-year history. He was probably one of the best prepared for the job. As chief scout he was responsible for getting all the players on the team but two, and he had even scouted one of them in college.

The big man the Knicks had been seeking for so long, Willis Reed, was drafted out of Grambling College in 1964, though it was not until Holzman took over that the proper use was made of Reed.

In 1965 the Knicks acquired Princeton All-American Bill Bradley, Dave Stallworth of Wichita State, and Dick Van Arsdale of Indiana. In 1966 they drafted Cazzie Russell of Michigan; the following year Walt Frazier of Southern Illinois, Phil Jackson of North Dakota, and Mike Riordan of Providence.

Holzman established control of the team immediately. At his first practice he fined five players for being late. "I was prepared to work hard and I expected the players to do the same thing," he said then.

He continued to schedule practices on nearly every day off and told the players that their Christmas that year would have to come in July. He concentrated 80 per cent of practice time on defense and he not only told the players what he wanted, he showed them through individual instruction.

On offense, Holzman gave the players about 20 plays, each with variations. Almost all were designed to free one player for an uncontested shot and the Knicks' motto became: "Hit the open man."

The team was also quick to borrow plays from other teams. By the time the Knicks were through practicing them over and over, the Knicks usually ran the plays better than the team from which they had borrowed the plays.

In addition, Holzman encouraged his players to suggest plays that might work. Bradley and Jackson, both good strategists, were the most frequent contributors.

"I always wanted the players to feel free to suggest new things for our offense," Holzman has said. "Then they'll break their necks to make them work. If they don't use their basketball intelligence, all their years in the game become an untapped spring that's going to waste.

"I don't mind telling you that our team won many games because of suggestions the players came up with. They made me a better coach."

The team responded right from the start. "It was very easy to play for Red," said Willis Reed after his retirement. "He handled us with respect, so we felt the same way toward him. Everyone plays best for someone he respects.

"For another thing, he knew us all through his scouting — even Dick Barnett. Red had scouted Barnett when Dick was still at Tennessee State. The point is that when Red took over, he knew his players' abilities and personalities better than most coaches did who'd been in the league for several years."

Holzman immediately began to give Walt Frazier more playing time and Frazier improved rapidly. The next season, the Knicks finished third with a 54-28 record and Holzman was starting to use Bradley more often.

That same season was more notable, however, because of a trade General Manager Eddie Donovan made. It gave Holzman the material he needed to mold the Knicks into a champion.

Donovan sent center Walt Bellamy and guard Butch Komives to Detroit for Dave DeBusschere, a bruising 6-foot, 6-inch forward. That enabled Holzman to move Reed from forward to center and give Frazier even more playing time. And with DeBusschere playing his power game at one forward, the Knicks could afford to use Bradley, an excellent shooter but weak rebounder, at the other forward.

The next season, 1969-1970, was the Knicks' glory year. They won 60 games, including a record 18 in a row (since broken) and faced Los Angeles for the NBA championship. The teams split the first six games of the championship series, the Knicks losing the sixth after Willis Reed was sidelined. But in the seventh game, Reed, helped by Carbocane and Cortisone shots, made a dramatic return.

Though limping badly because of a painful hip injury, Reed, following Holzman's strategy, destroyed the Laker defense. The first two times the Knicks brought the ball down court, Reed got the ball. He hobbled away from Wilt Chamberlain and hit two uncontested one-hand shots from the top of the key. That forced Chamberlain to come outside, away from the basket, to guard Reed. By forcing Wilt outside, the Knicks opened up the middle so they could drive to the basket.

When Reed could finally no longer take the pain and left the game, there were still three and one-half minutes left in the first half. But New York led 61-37 and the championship was decided.

The following year the Knicks won the Eastern Division but were eliminated by Baltimore in the Eastern finals. The 1971-1972 Knicks were second in the East, but battled through to the finals. There, with Reed and DeBusschere both hurt, they lost in five games to the Lakers.

In 1972-1973 the Knicks won the championship again. Bolstered by the additions of guard Earl Monroe and center Jerry Lucas via trades, the Knicks won 57 of 82 games and beat division champion Boston in the Eastern play-offs. They lost the first game of the finals to the Lakers and then won the next four for the title.

The Knicks lost Reed the next season but still managed to win 49 games and finish second in the East. Boston beat them in five games in the play-offs and went on to the championship.

The Knicks who took the floor for the 1974-1975 season were barely recognizable. Gone were DeBusschere,

Reed, and Lucas, all retired, as well as Dean Meminger, a guard whom Holzman used to spot-play with brilliant results. There were no adequate replacements. The Knicks struggled to a 40-42 record and fell to 38-44 in the 1975-1976 season.

But while the Knicks were on top, they set a standard and a style that has been copied by every good team that developed after them. Boston, Golden State, Washington, Cleveland — all boasted overall team play and stingy defenses.

Coaches were trying to copy Holzman, too. He became acknowledged as a master at calling critical times-out, at substituting players in the final three minutes, at figuring out individual match-ups which worked to the Knicks' advantage.

But while others followed, Holzman remained the leader. Said DeBusschere upon his retirement, "Red may well be one of the best coaches in the game, if not the best.

"There is more to the game of basketball than coaching or manipulating players, and this man has it. It's difficult to describe except to say that he blends his coaching with every ingredient of life itself."

14

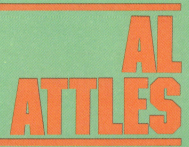

AL ATTLES

Before the 1974-1975 NBA season started, the league's coaches picked the Golden State Warriors to finish fourth in the Pacific Division. The reasoning was that coach Al Attles had All-Star forward Rick Barry and little else.

Attles had lost four starters from the previous season. He had boldly traded away veteran center Nate Thurmond. Forward Cazzie Russell had played out his option. Guard Jim Barnett had been taken in the expansion draft by New Orleans and Clyde Lee had been lost in a complicated deal that completed an earlier trade. Then, just before the season started, guard Jeff Mullins, the only player other than Barry with proven ability, broke a finger.

That left Attles with Barry and a collection of rookies, castoffs, and nice guys. "Rick Barry and the no-names" some wise guys were calling them. Sounded more like a rock group than a basketball team.

But Attles, who has always been a Warrior, has also always been a fighter. He began to whip his team into shape.

Prior to the season, the Warriors played a series of exhibitions with Los Angeles and Laker assistant coach John Barnhill recalls the Warriors' development:

"You could see that Al was putting their team together," Barnhill told reporters. "They were going to go out and hustle a team to death. He just seemed to lift them right up and make them go, and that's a tribute to Attles the coach.

"A couple of their guys were telling me about practice coming to a close one day. 'How do you feel?' Al asked them. 'Fine,' said one. 'That's good,' Al said. 'You run two more laps and you'll feel even better.' They enjoy it. He makes it fun. And that's how you make a good team go, the way Attles does it."

And go they did. All the way to the NBA championship.

First the Warriors won their division title with a 48-34 record. Then they began to knock off teams in the play-offs. First

Seattle, then Chicago. Suddenly, they were in the finals against the heavily-favored Washington Bullets, a team of superstars.

The finals would be short and sweet the experts said. Washington in five games, they said. The experts were half right. But it was Golden State in four. In three of the four games of the championship series Washington jumped to big leads — 16, 14, and 13 points. The Warriors battled back in every one for victory. No one believed it but the Warriors.

Then over the summer the Milwaukee Bucks traded All-Everything center Kareem Abdul-Jabbar to Los Angeles. The experts responded by showing that, in addition to other failings, they also possessed short memories. The Lakers will win the title with Jabbar, the experts said. Easy, they said.

The mistake the experts made is that they didn't pay attention. They still thought that Golden State was Rick Barry and four guys named Joe, that their championship was a fluke, an accident.

That kind of thinking was fine as far as Attles was concerned because he knew it meant that no one yet had caught on.

In the first place, he would take the championship even if it was an accident, which it wasn't. Second, having Rick Barry on your side is not something to sneer at. And third, Attles did not have four guys named Joe — he had 11. And that was the key to the whole thing.

The reason was simple. There were a number of teams around the league whose starting fives were better than the Warriors' first five. But the NBA allows 12-man rosters and Attles used every man; in nearly every game. And no 12-man team in the league was as good as Golden State.

"If you have players who can play," Attles has explained his philosophy, "there's no reason why they should just sit there night after night. We don't have that one big rebounder. What we have is eight guys, getting eight rebounds each. Everybody is involved."

And no one was named Joe. Instead they were called Phil Smith, Jamaal Wilkes, Derrek Dickey, Clifford Ray, George Johnson, Charles Johnson, Dwight Davis, Charles Dudley, Robert Hawkins, and the newest of the group, Gus Williams.

What these players did was kill a team with determined, aggressive play; use a little muscle and finesse; and run, run, run. In that, they were a lot like their coach.

Attles arrived in the NBA when the Warriors, then in Philadelphia, drafted him on the fifth round out of North Carolina A&T. He was just six-feet tall, but he had a reputation for aggressiveness and for sacrificing himself for the team.

"I expected to stay long enough to get a ticket back to my home in Newark," Attles has recalled. Instead, he became a rarity in the NBA, staying 17 years with one club.

Attles was rarely one to get into the headlines, unless it was because of one of his celebrated fights, usually with a much larger player. He once had 17 assists in a game and in his best season he averaged 11.2 points.

One of the best games Attles ever played came one night when he sank all eight of

his field goal tries and made his only free throw. Even that night, however, he didn't make the headlines. For that was the night Wilt Chamberlain scored 100 points for the Warriors.

But Attles stayed because he was a battler and because he played good defense.

Lenny Wilkens, now the Portland coach, remembers Attles well. "He was on you like a glove all the time," recalled Wilkens. "We came into the league the same year, and when he guarded me I knew I had to have my full concentration."

And Tom Meschery, now the Houston coach but a former teammate, remembers Attles as "the toughest single fighter I ever saw in the league." Attles was so tough that in his 11 years as a player he earned the nickname "The Destroyer."

He showed that combativeness in the 1975 finals when Mike Riordan of the Bullets tried to pick a fight with Barry, apparently hoping to have Barry kicked out of the game. Barry, a noted fighter himself, walked away, but it took three players to drag Attles off Riordan.

20　Attles moved from player to coach in January 1970 when club owner Franklin Mieuli practically begged him to take the job. Attles three times declined to take the job before finally relenting and succeeding George Lee.

"I was an average black player with no technical experience," Attles said then. "I just didn't think I was mentally prepared to deal with 12 different personalities." He did it, he said, "because Franklin had always been good to me."

The team he took over finished with an 8-22 record under him, but he hasn't had a loser since. His 298-224 regular season record for a percentage of .570 makes him one of the most successful young coaches in the game.

Though the Warriors were unable to repeat as NBA champions in 1975-1976, losing to Phoenix in the Western Division finals, Golden State had the combination of youth, experience, and coaching to be a title contender for many years.

BILL SHARMAN

Bill Sharman's coaching history reads like that of a miracle worker. In almost every job, he has taken teams that were losers and turned them into champions.

But things suddenly turned around after Sharman led the Los Angeles Lakers to their only NBA title in 1971-1972. Four years later Sharman found himself in need of a miracle.

No one, however, was betting that Sharman wouldn't be able to find one. The key to his success has always been dedication, concentration and hard work.

At the start of the 1975-1976 season, Red Auerbach noted that four former Celtics were coaching NBA teams. The Boston Celtics general manager called Sharman "the hardest worker and the most dedicated. And he has the most money behind him."

The money behind him was one of the biggest pressures Sharman faced. For Los Angeles owner Jack Kent Cooke does not like to lose. Cooke had decided, it was said, that the only answer to the Lakers' problems would be a new coach. In August 1976, Cooke named former Laker superstar Jerry West the Los Angeles coach. Sharman was named assistant general manager of the Lakers.

The Sharman story had its beginning on May 25, 1926, in Porterville, California. As a youth on the California playgrounds, Sharman was an all-around athlete. But he preferred basketball because it was the only game a boy could play by himself. All he needed was a basket and a ball.

At the University of Southern California, Sharman was outstanding both on the basketball court and the baseball diamond. After college he played briefly in the Brooklyn Dodgers' farm system. Though he never played in a major league game, he was in the Dodger dugout the day the New York Giants' Bobby Thomson hit baseball's most dramatic home run in 1951. That beat the Dodgers for the pennant.

But Sharman switched uniforms, breaking into pro basketball with the old Washington Caps before becoming a Celtic. In Boston he teamed with guard

Bob Cousy to become one of the all-time great backcourt combinations.

As a Celtic, Sharman led the team in scoring for four straight years, beginning in 1955-1956. He was the team's best free throw shooter for 10 straight years and had the best shooting percentage for two seasons. He led the league in free throw percentage for seven seasons and is the leading free throw percentage shooter in play-off history with 91.1%

For those accomplishments Sharman was named an All-Pro seven times and played in 10 NBA All-Star games. He won the game's Most Valuable Player award in 1955.

Sharman's ability at the free throw line is evidence of his concentration, dedication, and hard work because there is no other way to become a good free throw shooter. When he went into the coaching ranks in the American Basketball League (ABL) in 1961, he took those traits with him. He started as coach of the Los Angeles Jets, but the team folded at midseason. He then took over the Cleveland Pipers and led the team from last place to the league title. The next season the entire ABL folded.

After two years coaching in college at California State University at Lost Angeles, and two more as a basketball broadcaster, Sharman joined the NBA head coaching

ranks with San Francisco in 1966. The season before the Warriors had a 35-45 record. Sharman made them winners immediately. The team finished his first season with a 44-37 record and barely lost in the championship finals to Wilt Chamberlain's Philadelphia team.

Despite his success with the Warriors, Sharman was not popular with the players. He expected them to work as hard as he did. He held practices on the day of a game and had countless team meetings, going over films of the opposition much like a football coach.

When Warrior superstar Rick Barry jumped to the American Basketball Association, reportedly partly because of Sharman, team owner Franklin Mieuli became angry. He refused to rehire Sharman and the coach followed Barry into the ABA.

In his second year at Utah, Sharman took that team, a team with no real stars to the ABA championship. But he didn't stay long. He learned that the Lakers were looking for a coach, applied for the job, and got it.

At Los Angeles Sharman walked into a pressure job unlike any in the NBA. The Lakers had lost in 7 play-off finals in their 11 years in L.A. And the team had three of the greatest, but oldest, stars in the game

Elgin Baylor, then 37, Wilt Chamberlain, 35, and Jerry West, 33. All had egos which matched their abilities.

Despite the decline of his aging players, Sharman was determined to turn the team into a fast-break club. "That's the basketball I learned from Red Auerbach," he told reporters, "and it's what I teach.

"You have to hustle every minute of every game and you have to sacrifice yourself unselfishly for the team. No other sport except boxing can compare with basketball in the importance of conditioning."

Since his affair with Barry, Sharman had learned a great deal about handling men. He met with the three stars, informed them of his plans, and received their cooperation.

Even Chamberlain, often viewed as a problem player, was on his good behavior. "He did not miss a single practice all season," recalled Sharman. "He grumbled a bit, but we did not have a serious disagreement."

Baylor was a different problem. He was no longer the player he once had been and Sharman had a young player, Jim McMillian, who could play the running game better. Sharman talked to Baylor, said he wanted to have him come off the bench. A few days later Baylor announced

his retirement. The day McMillian replaced him in the lineup, the Lakers roared off on a 33-game winning streak, an NBA record.

Sharman calls that 1971-1972 team, which finished with a 69-13 record, the best over a single season he has ever seen. "We had beautiful balance in McMillian and Happy Hairston up front," he has said, "Wilt at center and West and Gail Goodrich at the guards. We had a reliable bench. Every player complemented every other player."

That team went on to win the NBA title and Sharman became the first coach ever to win championships in the three major basketball leagues, the NBA being the only surviving league. The 1972 NBA championship also brought Sharman Coach of the Year recognition.

But it was not the start for the Lakers, it was the finish. The Lakers won 60 games the following season only to lose in the finals to the New York Knicks. Then, in quick succession, Wilt jumped to the ABA, West missed almost a full season with injuries and then retired, and Jim McMillian was traded to Buffalo.

While his team was falling apart, Sharman was also experiencing personal problems. He lost his voice about six weeks before the end of the championship season. The condition did not totally clear up for two years.

And, in the summer of 1972, it was discovered his second wife, Dorothy, was seriously ill. She suffered, as did Sharman, for the next three years, before she died.

Following her death in September 1975, Sharman plunged back into the sport in an effort to make a new start. The Lakers, who had slipped in four years from a title to a 30-52 record in 1974-1975, traded away four young players to Milwaukee for Kareem Abdul-Jabbar.

The experts predicted that would be the start of something new for L. A., that the Lakers would win the championship.

They were wrong. All the trade proved was that in the NBA one superstar cannot win a championship by himself. Jabbar was named the NBA's Most Valuable Player for 1975-1976 but his teammates gave him little support.

Meanwhile, the four players the Lakers traded away made Milwaukee strong enough to win the weak Midwest Division and make the play-offs. The Lakers could finish no better than fourth in the Pacific Division with a 40-42 record. They did not make the play-offs.

And Bill Sharman, once hailed as the team's savior, was , several weeks later, off the bench and in the Lakers' front office. It was a strange position for a miracle worker to be in and only time would tell if he had another one left in him.

K.C. JONES

The most disappointing team in the NBA during the 1975-1976 season was the Washington Bullets and the most disappointed coach was K.C. Jones, their coach.

The disappointment for K.C. actually had started at the end of the previous season. In 1974-1975 he had led the Bullets to a 60-22 record (only 12 other teams had ever won that many games before) and into the finals of the NBA play-offs. There the Bullets were expected to demolish the Golden State Warriors, a team of four unknowns surrounding Rick Barry.

But in one of the most unusual championship series in history, the Bullets collapsed. They lost leads of 16, 14, and 13 points in three of the four games and Golden State became only the third team in history to sweep a championship series.

No one could explain what had happened to the Bullets. On paper Jones had one of the strongest teams in the league. For most of the season he had molded his players' individual abilities so well that it often seemed that they were unbeatable.

For example, the Bullets were the second best defensive team in the league and the fifth best offensive team. Forward Elvin Hayes was the seventh leading scorer, center Wes Unseld was the top average rebounder, and guard Kevin Porter was the leading assist man.

But the Bullets' fine team play disintegrated during the championship series and Jones, who had been hailed for his ability during the regular season, suddenly was being criticized.

Adversity, however, was nothing new to the Bullets' coach. He had been a scrapper all his life.

K.C. was born 43 years ago in Taylor, Texas, and christened with the initial K.C. in honor of his father. His father was a postal worker and by the time K.C. was 12 he had lived in five different cities.

Not until the Jones family settled in San Francisco did K.C.'s life become more normal. He had experienced racial prejudice in the Southwest but at Commerce High School he was surrounded by Mexicans, Chinese, and other blacks and he was no longer a standout. Except in sports.

"When I left high school," he once recalled, "I was the highest scorer in the city. But then I grew three inches that summer and lost my shot . . . I don't know why."

Though he made All-Northern California in both football and basketball, he didn't make the list of any college recruiters.

"I didn't really care," K.C. has said. "Coming from where I did, in the ghetto, I just figured I was going to get a job at the post office, buy a car, and that was going to be it. College never really entered my mind."

Finally, however, he received four scholarship offers. He chose to stay close to home and attend the University of San Francisco. K.C. made no headlines in his first two years at USF and, in fact, he almost died from an abdominal infection when he was a sophomore.

But when he recovered things were different. He and teammate Bill Russell led USF to 60 straight victories and two NCAA basketball championships (1955, 1956). He and Russell then led the U.S. Olympic team to victory at Melbourne, Australia. Afterward K.C. went into the army for two years.

After he completed his military duty, Pete Rozelle, now the commissioner of the National Football League, convinced K.C. to try pro football. Rozelle, who was then a publicity man for the Los Angeles Rams, had known K.C. when both were at USF. K.C. tried out as a cornerback but abandoned the sport when the Rams wanted him to play with a severe charley horse.

K.C. then called coach Red Auerbach at Boston and asked if he could have a tryout with the Celtics. The tryout turned into a nine-year job with the Celtics.

"All I did was hustle and run," K.C. has said. "I sat on the bench for four years — the first couple of years I played five minutes a game."

During that span the Celtics, with Bob Cousy as the playmaker and Russell at center, won four championships. Then Cousy retired and K.C. replaced him. K.C. quickly became the team's playmaker but,

more important, along with Russell he became one of the game's greatest defensive players. The Celtics went on to win four more NBA titles.

When K.C. finally retired, he became head coach at Brandeis University. But the experience was a disaster because the school did not give scholarships. He then became an assistant at Harvard and later joined Laker head coach Bill Sharman, a former Celtic teammate, as his assistant. That year the Lakers won their only championship.

After that K.C. became head coach of San Diego, an expansion team in the ABA. Though the club had only a 30-54 record, it was good enough to get into the play-offs.

Following the 1972-1973 season, the Bullets fired Gene Shue as coach and asked K.C. to replace him. K.C. jumped at the chance.

With the Bullets, K.C. applied to his job all the things he had learned as a Celtic.

"Respect, player to player, player to coach, and coach to player," K.C. once told reporters, "that's the thing I got out of the Celtics." His coaching philosophy remained simple: fast break, look for the open man, and play defense. "It's just realizing that fundamental basketball wins games," K.C. said.

Though center Wes Unseld was in and out of the lineup all that first season because of a bad knee, K.C. led the Bullets to a 47-35 record, first place in their division, and into the play-offs before they were eliminated.

The important thing, however, was the impression he made on his players. "The pro coach, most importantly, has to know what makes certain players tick and have the ability to teach both individually and collectively," Mike Riordan told reporters. "K.C. has impressed me with his knowledge of the game and his ability to deal with problems."

The following season, K.C. led the Bullets to their dream season only to see it turn into a nightmare at the end.

Though when training camp opened for the next season, Jones had said, "I replayed the Golden State series the whole summer," he had found no answers. Still it didn't seem as if it would matter. The Bullets appeared even stronger for 1975-1976.

The team had traded Kevin Porter to Detroit for guard Dave Bing, the third leading active scorer in the NBA. Bing figured to make the offense that much more powerful.

But the Bullets appeared as if they had not gotten over the Golden State series the previous spring. They lacked the team play they had displayed the previous season and were inconsistent.

"I was down," K.C. said late in the season. "I was really low at one point, but all I could do was go to practice and work hard. You've got to keep getting up when you're down or it's all over."

But no matter how hard K.C. worked, the Bullets seemed unconcerned. They finished the season with a 48-34 record, second to Cleveland in the East's Central Division. It was the first time in six years that the team had failed to win the division championship. To make matters worse, Cleveland then eliminated the Bullets in the quarter-final play-offs.

K.C., who was in the last year of a three-year contract, had the second best winning percentage in the league over that period. But critics said he wasn't tough enough with the players. And when a team doesn't live up to expectations, its owners do not get rid of the team, they get rid of the coach. Which is what the Bullets did on May 7, 1976. They replaced him with a noted disciplinarian, Dick Motta, who was coaching the Chicago Bulls.

The players reacted angrily to the firing of K.C.

"That's pathetic," Elvin Hayes told reporters. "What happened this year just wasn't his fault. It was the fault of the players on the court."

Team captain Wes Unseld agreed. "If we, as individual players, had put the team before ourselves, things would have been different."

K.C.'s assistant, Bernie Bickerstaff, also backed up his former boss. "If it hadn't been for K.C.," Bickerstaff told reporters, "the Bullets would have folded long ago. But he never panicked and he kept everyone else from panicking when things started going really bad.

"We don't have any bad feelings about the way we have done things here. If you give it your best shot, you can be satisfied as a person even if you don't win it all, and I think we gave it our best."

But, then K.C. Jones doesn't know any other way.

BILL FITCH

Bill Fitch and his Cleveland Cavaliers are no longer a laughing matter around the NBA. Nowhere save in Cleveland, that is, where Cavalier fans are so happy they can hardly wipe the grins off their faces.

The reason is simple. Fitch, the only coach the team has ever had, turned a team that was once the butt of jokes around the league into one of the most promising franchises in the NBA. And the Cavs can only get better.

But the outlook was far from that bright when Fitch took over as Cleveland coach for the team's first season in 1970. He had left a promising job at the University of Minnesota to coach one of the league's three new franchises. He knew the early years would be a struggle. They were even worse — they were a disaster.

Through it all, however, Fitch had a quick smile and an even quicker quip. He became known as the NBA's answer to

Bob Hope. Without his sense of humor, he might not have survived.

The Cavaliers were losers from the start. In the player draft they lost a coin flip with the other new teams, Portland and Buffalo, and had to pick third. And before the start of their first season, they lost a scheduling battle to the Ice Capades and spent the first 12 days on the road. They topped even that by losing their first 15 games.

"It was a nightmare," Fitch has said. "When I finally got some sleep, I dreamt I was awake."

But things were slow to improve. After winning their first game, the Cavaliers went on to lose their next 12. "We're the only team to lose nine in a row," Fitch said then, "and then go into a slump."

The rest of that first season was more of the same. The Cavaliers finished fourth in the Central Division (the first of four straight finishes at that position) with a 15-67 record. And Fitch continued to supply the one-liners.

"We're the only team who could play back-to-back games on 'What's My Line' and stump the panel," he'd say . . . "I feel like a guy whose ship came in only to find there was a dock strike . . . I phoned Dial-A-Prayer, but when they found out who it was, they hung up."

Fitch kept people laughing so much they almost forgot how bad his team was. But he didn't and he was determined things would change.

The 40-year-old native of Cedar Rapids, Iowa, learned to hate losing on the playgrounds when he was growing up. "When I was a kid," he has said, "the guys I played with weren't exactly good winners. I can't remember losing and having any of them shake my hand. You were humiliated in losing. They rubbed salt in your wounds.

"Losing like that develops three things. It develops fear — fear of losing. It becomes a pride factor. And then it becomes a challenge. I guess if I have a loose wire, it's that I have a lot of pride."

Fitch carried his spirit of competition into the coaching ranks, where it took him to bigger and better jobs. He coached at his alma mater, Coe College, in his home town, then went on to Creighton University in Omaha. Next stop was for five years at the University of North Dakota where his 1965 team finished fourth in the small college playoffs.

From there Fitch went to Bowling Green, a mediocre team when he arrived. He took it to the Mid-America Conference championship and a playoff berth in the NCAA before losing to Marquette. For that he was named Ohio Coach of the Year.

Minnesota grabbed Fitch then and though he didn't perform any miracles with the Gophers, who were only a .500 team, he did revive interest in the basketball program. After he departed, one of his top recruits, Jim Brewer, led the Gophers to their first conference championship in over 30 years.

Fitch was persuaded to leave Minnesota to take the Cleveland job by the team's owner and general manager, Nick Mileti. Mileti, who had known Fitch at Bowling Green, presented the job as a challenge to him. It was a challenge Fitch couldn't turn down, but he warned Mileti at the time, "My name's not Houdini."

The first year was the worst because Fitch was new to the league. He chose to draft for the future and those youths and the collection of castoffs from other teams that made up the Cavaliers were expected to be losers. They were.

Still there were laughs. One Cavalier, John Warren, once completed a dazzling drive with some neat footwork and a layup. Then he discovered he had made it in the wrong basket. Another player put his luggage on a plane to Chicago only to learn that the game was in Boston. Still another fell asleep on a plane and got locked up inside overnight.

"We couldn't make a basket, we couldn't rebound, and we didn't play defense," Fitch said of his team. "You might say we put it all together."

Fitch drafted Notre Dame's Austin Carr, the best collegian the previous season, and it appeared Cav fortunes were on the upswing. Then, during the summer, Carr broke his foot. He recovered, reported to training camp, and broke it again.

The Cavaliers finished their second season with a 23-59 record, were 32-50 the next season, and 29-53 the one after that. Through it all Fitch continued to build his team.

After the 1972-1973 season, he traded away John Johnson and Rick Roberson, two starters, to Portland for the rights to Brewer, the player he had recruited at Minnesota. When Brewer failed to become an instant star, the move was ridiculed. After the 1973-1974 season Fitch signed 6-foot-11 center Jim Chones, who had failed to live up to expectations in the then rival American Basketball Association (ABA). Chones had a reputation of being stubborn, lazy, and timid.

"I didn't know where I was or where I was going," Chones has said. "Coach Fitch gave me a chance. We had long talks and he told me that if I played hard enough, he would keep me on the floor. In the ABA I hurt myself because I didn't have what you'd call a professional attitude."

Fitch changed that by immediately testing Chones. He yelled at him, taunted him, goaded him.

"The other players loved him," Fitch has said. "I spent so much time hollering at Jim, the other players got off easy."

Chones responded by giving the Cavaliers solid center play, rebounding, scoring (a 14.5 average), and passing. That season the Cavaliers finished two games under .500, 40-42, and missed the play-offs on the final day of the season.

That set the stage for 1975-1976. After the Cavs lost 11 of their first 17 games, Fitch made another controversial move. He traded two promising young players to Chicago for Roland Garrett and veteran center Nate Thurmond. The 33-year-old Thurmond was thought to be washed up, but was the key to the deal.

Thurmond played 16 to 20 minutes a game, and allowed Fitch to rest Chones or Brewer without hurting the team. The Cavs, thus strengthened, won the Central Division with a 49-33 record and then eliminated Washington in the first round of the play-offs in seven games.

The fans reacted as though the Cavs were giving away money at The Coliseum, the team's sparkling new home in a Cleveland suburb. All through the Washington series the team set attendance records, drawing crowds in excess of 21,000. That from a team that averaged 2,500 in its first season playing in an aging midtown arena.

But the team's dreams suffered a severe jolt when Chones broke his foot before the start of its next series with eventual champion Boston. Without Chones, the Cavs were eliminated in six games. A disappointed Fitch could only say, "If we had had Jim Chones, we could have beaten anybody."

Strangely, though the Cavaliers had arrived after six years, Fitch wasn't happy. Though he had been named Coach of the Year during the playoffs, he was reported to be in a dispute with Mileti. He reportedly even hired a lawyer to see if he could get out of the final two years of his contract at Cleveland.

Accepting challenges, it seemed, just comes natural to Fitch.

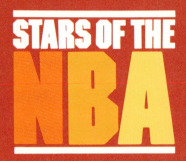

STARS OF THE NBA

THE GUARDS
THE COACHES
THE CENTERS
THE FORWARDS